(DEFINITELY) the BEST DOGS OF ALL TIME

JADAN CARROLL lives in Melbourne and has worked in music management, entertainment publicity and festival programming and production for the past 10 years. He does not own a dog. This is his first book.

MOLLY DYSON is an Australian illustrator based in Berlin. Since completing a Bachelor of Fine Art at Victorian College of the Arts in 2010, her work has been featured in publications including *The Lifted Brow*, *Frankie*, *Vice*, and *Merry Jane*.

(DEFINITELY) the BEST DOGS OF ALL TIME

Jadan Carroll

with illustrations by
Molly Dyson

SCRIBE
Melbourne • London

For Fiona.
Dream dog. Life coach. Undercover pig.
And for Perrin and Evan, who keep
me updated on her goings on.

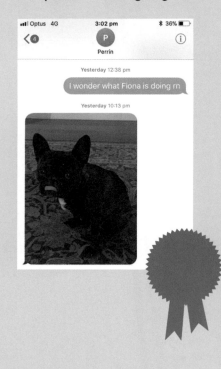

CONTENTS

Introduction

Dogs are the best. I was terrified of them as a kid. My grandparents owned a great bounding Boxer named Zorro. Growing up, my mum and I lived with them for several years, and every day after school, Zorro would race to the front gate to meet me — jumping up to put one giant paw on each of my shoulders and licking my face with his huge slobbering tongue. I was convinced he was trying to eat me.

It wasn't until years later that I realised that he was just saying hi, and that he'd missed me, and that for years I'd spurned his daily loving greeting by squealing in his face and running away. I was a very sensitive kid. Sorry, Zorro.

History is filled with stories about so many wonderful dogs. Tales of unconditional love, companionship, adventure, playfulness, heroism, loyalty. And usually we don't deserve any of it. As a species, we've shot dogs into space, sent them to war, subjected them to horrible cruelty and neglect. And they still love and trust us.

They are so great.

The way that they absolutely could not for a second

consider that we may have just pretended to throw the ball, and it couldn't possibly just be behind our backs.

The way they sit panting in contentedness after a long run, tails wagging, their eyes half-closed, huge grins on their faces.

Are they really smiling? I hope so. What are they thinking? I bet it's very deep and funny. What do they dream about? Is life real or is our entire existence the construct of a dog's imagination, the daydream of a great celestial Labrador dozing in the warmth of a giant sun in a parallel dimension? I'm clearly not the first person to wonder this (see 'Bouncer', pp. 66-69).

But which of them are the best, the bravest, the kindest, the most inspiring, the all-round goodest? And how could this even be decided?

In 2017, *Guardian* Australia ran a poll on the best birds. They focused on bird breeds, rather than actual or historical birds — if they'd done the latter, Iggy Pop's cockatoo, Biggy Pop, would have to be a shoo-in (Instagram — look him up). And they confined the voting field to species native to Australia. It was the most exciting thing to happen in Australia all year. There were so many delightful birds to choose from. The southern cassowary, the splendid fairywren, the superb lyrebird, THE EMU.

But we cooked it.

The powerful owl was disqualified due to suspicious voting activity, which was blamed on Russian hackers (seriously).

Hordes of apathetic voters trolled the poll and threw their weight behind the white ibis, colloquially known as the 'bin chicken'. It came second.

In the end the magpie won — not because it was the best, but because it was associated with a football team.

Democracy doesn't work, and, as a society, we can't be trusted with these tasks.

But it's down to *someone* to decide the best dogs of all time, and so I've taken this upon myself.

For this book I've chosen to focus on real-life historical dogs, contemporary dogs, dogs of the internet, and dogs from mythology. To include all of the amazing fictional dogs from throughout the entire history of human story-telling, film, books, and cartoons would require a much longer book. Also, licensing fees are astronomical.

I don't own a dog; I'm not a dog expert ('dogspert' is a word that I have heard used, but I refuse to use it outside of parentheses); I have no dog-related qualifications; and I've never written a book, let alone a book about dogs. With all that said, the dogs in this book are absolutely, unequivocally, one hundred per cent, definitely the best dogs of all time.

And if you don't agree with me, that's totally fine. Write me a letter. Make your own list. Or write your own dog book. It's bound to be excellent. Dogs are the best.

and now...

The
**BEST
DOGS**
of All Time

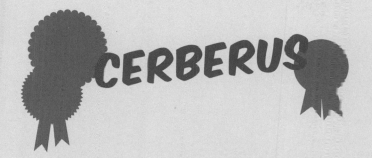

CERBERUS

The much misunderstood, multi-headed hound of Hades, Cerberus was tasked with standing guard at the gates of the Underworld, preventing the dead from leaving.

By all accounts he was really, really good at his crucial work, protecting the world from the zombie apocalypse.

Cerberus was from a large family of multi-headed siblings including Chimera, Hydra, and Medusa. It's uncertain exactly how many heads Cerberus had: some texts say two, some three, and at least one puts his head count at one hundred, which seems slightly over the top. He's mostly depicted as having three heads, though — an extra-special number of heads for a dog.

Cerberus's older brother, Orthrus, was a two-headed dog who guarded the cattle of Geryon. Orthrus was also a very good guard dog; it ran in the family. That is, until Orthrus was savagely killed by Heracles (known to the Romans as Hercules), while the 'hero' carried out his tenth labour, stealing the very cattle that Orthrus was tasked to guard.

Then, for his twelfth and final labour — or for no

other reason than the fact that he was a massive show-off — Heracles captured Cerberus, dragged him up from the Underworld, and cruelly paraded him through Greece in chains, jeered at and mocked by townsfolk. Cerberus may have been a 'monster', but we all know who the real monster of this story is (it's Heracles).

Following Heracles's reign of terror upon his family, Cerberus showed up in a cameo role as 'Fluffy' in the Harry Potter franchise. So maybe things worked out okay for him.

Heracles showing off; being a jerk.

SIRIUS
Dog Star

Astrological Dog. Celestial Dog. Extra-terrestrial Dog. Sirius is the brightest star in our night sky and known colloquially as the 'Dog Star'. It is located in the constellation *Canis Major* — the Greater Dog.

Across the world and throughout history, many cultures have made a canine connection with Sirius.

In Greek mythology, the season following its rising was known as the 'dog days' of summer, and, through the pure Power of Dog, Sirius would bring about weakness in men, arousal in women, and madness in dogs.

The Pawnee of North America referred to it as 'Wolf Star' or 'Coyote Star'; to the Inuit, further north in Alaska, it was known as 'Moon Dog'; while to the ancient Chinese, it was 'Celestial Wolf'.

Commonly, Sirius is depicted as the hound of Orion, the giant hunter of Greek legend, whose three-starred belt lights the sky nearby.

Twenty-five times brighter than our Sun and twice the size, Sirius is unquestionably the most powerful dog in this book.

CHINESE ZODIAC DOG

Dogs have further heavenly representations in the skies of Chinese mythology. Lunar and solar eclipses were said to be created by the great black dog Tiangu, who would chase the moon and the sun and eat them. The god Zhang Xian, the eternal enemy of Tiangu, stands guard on earth, driving off the dog with his bow and arrows, and forcing Tiangu to spit the moon or the sun back out, again and again.

The Dog is also the eleventh sign of the 12-year Chinese zodiac cycle, in which each year is represented by one of 12 different animals. The cycle roughly corresponds with the 11.86-year orbit of the planet Jupiter around the Sun.

The animals are said to have competed in The Great Race, swimming across a river for their place in the Chinese calendar. Although he was the best swimmer of them all, the Dog placed second-last. He'd had so much fun playing in the water that he'd forgotten the race was even happening. Those born in the Year of the Dog are said to share the dog's traits: loyalty; playfulness; and a complete inability to focus on the task at hand.

NIETZSCHE'S DOG

existential dog

The unsung muse of one of the nineteenth century's most questioning and complicated minds.

> 'I have given a name to my pain and call it "dog". It is just as faithful, just as obtrusive and shameless, just as entertaining, just as clever as any other dog.'
>
> **Friedrich Nietzsche**

No one is sure if this dog actually existed.

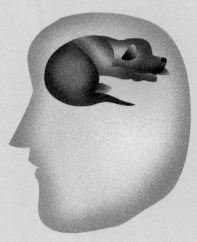

GREYFRIARS BOBBY

Perhaps the most famous terrier in Scotland, and the subject of at least one novel, two films, and several entire history books, Greyfriars Bobby was a small Skye Terrier from Edinburgh.

The legend goes that local policeman John Gray took on Bobby as a pet to keep him company on his lonely night-watch beat. Local residents came to know the pair well as the nightwatch-man and his tiny, bouncing (though hardly intimidating) terrier became a regular sight on the streets of Edinburgh.

When John died of tuberculosis in 1858 and was buried in Greyfriars Kirkyard, his faithful companion Bobby refused to leave his side. Bobby kept constant guard by John's grave for more than 14 years.

Statue of Greyfriars Bobby. Look at those kind and wise eyes.

The story of the little dog's undying devotion would soon spread across Scotland, and, in time, huge crowds would flock to see Bobby camped out by John's grave.

When a local by-law decreed that all dogs in the city of Edinburgh would be required to be licensed or face being put down, the Lord Provost of Edinburgh, Sir William Chambers, adopted Bobby, paid his license, and gifted him a fancy brass collar.

Soon after Bobby's death in 1872, Baroness Angela Georgina Burdett-Coutts paid for a fountain depicting Bobby to be built in his honour at Greyfriars Kirkyard.

To this day, tourists continue to visit Bobby's grave, often leaving sticks. For him to fetch.

Tiny dog. Huge heart. There, I said it.

HERE LIES

JOHN GRAY

MASTERPIECE

In the 1950s, an eccentric Russian entrepreneur and 'poodle fancier', Count Alexis Pulaski, opened Poodles, Incorporated on 52nd Street, Manhattan — a high-end dog boutique and salon, catering exclusively to poodles. The salon would come to be regarded as the Tiffany of dog stores, and holding court at its centre, on a small green velvet throne, was Masterpiece — Pulaski's prized Toy Poodle. Masterpiece would become famous the world over, and a regular fixture in New York society pages. He held the highest appraisal value of any dog in history. He was the poodle by which all other poodles were judged, and together, Pulaski and Masterpiece would topple the beagle from its perch as preferred pooch of the rich and famous.

But in 1953, the story of Masterpiece and Poodles, Inc. took a fascinating turn when Masterpiece was dognapped. A mysterious woman in red simply walked into the store, opened his enclosure, and walked out, with Masterpiece trailing obediently at her side. The news spread across the U.S. like wildfire. Police were on alert in more than a dozen states. Rewards were offered, fingers were pointed, and communists were blamed.

But Masterpiece would never be seen again.

> **Listen: Episode #84 of *Criminal* — a sensational half hour podcast episode devoted to Masterpiece and his mysterious disappearance.**

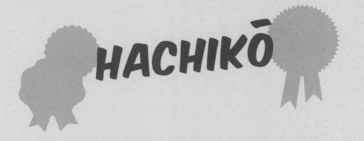

HACHIKŌ

Born in 1923 and taken in as a pet by Professor Hidesaburō Ueno in 1924, Hachikō was a Japanese Akita dog who lived in Shibuya. Each afternoon, Hachikō would greet Professor Ueno at Shibuya railway station, following the professor's commute home from work at The University of Tokyo.

When Professor Ueno died while giving a lecture in 1925, Hachikō was left at the station waiting. And for the next nine years, he would wait at the station every afternoon for his master, who would never return. By the time Hachikō died in 1935, he had become famous across Japan, and a national icon of loyalty and devotion. He was even present at the unveiling of a statue in his honour in 1934.

His story inspired numerous books and films including the 2009 movie *Hachi*, starring Richard Gere, and every year dog owners from across Japan converge on Shibuya station to commemorate his passing.

In 1994, the Culture Broadcasting Network in Japan aired a restored recording of Hachikō's bark, in what became a hugely publicised national event.

Mourners gather for the one-year anniversary of Hachikō's death.

In that moment, across the entire country, nothing could be heard except for the sound of Hachikō's mournful call for his long-lost owner, and the sound of millions of hearts shattering in unison.

He was so beautiful.

In Japan, a dog's bark is written as 'wan-wan' rather than 'woof-woof' or 'bow-wow'.

ODDBALL
and the penguin-protecting Maremmas of Middle Island

There is possibly nothing more heart-warming than stories of animals helping other animals, and the tale of an Australian Maremma who protected a waddle of penguins on an island off the coast of Warrnambool, Victoria, is top of the genre.

Oddball was the first dog in a pioneering project called 'Maremmas of Middle Island'. A local farmer named Swampy Marsh (!) had noticed that Maremmas made brilliant guardian dogs; they'd been protecting his chickens for years. Swampy suggested that they also be used to protect the local penguins during their breeding season, when they are particularly vulnerable to attacks from foxes and other animals.

In addition to having one of the greatest names of all time, Swampy Marsh also had great ideas. So in 2006, with her woolly white coat flowing in the cold coastal winds of Warrnambool, Swampy's trusty Maremma, Oddball, set off for Middle Island.

She nailed it, and instantly took to the task of protecting her new penguin friends from night-time predators. And although she swam home after three weeks because she got lonely, she also proved that Maremmas are the perfect penguin protectors. A crack team of these impressive creatures have been living on the island with the penguins ever since (cared for by the excellent people at the Middle Island Penguin Project).

The story of Oddball and the Maremmas of Middle Island took off around the world and inspired the 2015 film *Oddball*. Oddball passed away in 2017, leaving a crew of guardian angels/Maremmas to follow in her paw-prints.

A 'waddle' is a totally acceptable collective noun for a group of penguins; I've looked this up. 'Colony' and 'rookery' are also acceptable, but when 'waddle' is an option, the other two are actually not options.

DUKE
Mayor of Cormorant, Minnesota

This is Duke. He is a 10-year-old Great Pyrenees. He is also the Mayor of Cormorant, Minnesota. Yes. As his badge jauntily displays, Duke is the MAYOR of the small town of 1,000 people in Becker County.

He was first elected in 2014, and because the district holds elections annually, Duke has run for office every year since, winning four consecutive terms.

This is real. It's also entirely legal, as nowhere in local regulations does it specify that candidates need to be human.

Duke isn't the first dog, or even animal, to hold office. Nor is he the only one. Not even close.

Around the world, cats, dogs, mules, and goats have all been legitimately elected. In 1958, the people of São Paulo voted a rhinoceros named Cacareco to city council in protest at government corruption.

And, while Duke may only have won the last election from 12 votes cast (one was for his girlfriend Lassie, also a dog), others have won with far greater numbers.

BRYNNETH PAWLTRO
Mayor of Rabbit Hash

This is Brynneth Pawltro (actual name), the Pit-bull Mayor of Rabbit Hash, Kentucky.

Brynneth was elected with more than 3,000 votes. She replaced outgoing Mayor Lucy Lou, a Border Collie who had held office for MORE THAN EIGHT YEARS.

And while all of this is unquestionably adorable, the question should be asked — does this spate of dog mayors signal an ominous warning about the democratic process and its elected officials?

As a rule, the answer is probably, maybe, definitely, one hundred per cent yes.

"Hi, I'm the Mayor".
— Brynneth Pawltro

However, residents of Rabbit Hash say that their town is too small to warrant a human mayor, and that elections have been held as fundraising exercises for local projects, with voters charged $1 to cast a ballot. In fact, the election of Brynneth raised much-needed funds to enable Rabbit Hash Historical Society to rebuild the local general store, which had recently been destroyed by fire.

And that's beautiful. It's really, really neat. But this is how it begins, and soon we will be bowing down to the power of our new canine overlords, and it will be glorious.

Also, here's a picture of Max, the Mayor of Idyllwild, California, and YES HE'S WEARING A TIE.

A tie AND a medal.
Mayor Max of Idyllwild.

CHARLIE
Kennedy's dog

There have been many presidential dogs; in fact, nearly all of the U.S. presidents have owned pets, the majority being dogs. Roosevelt had a Scottish Terrier named Fala, whose statue stands at the Franklin D. Roosevelt Memorial in Washington. Obama had Bo and Sunny, George W. Bush had Spotty, and Clinton had Socks.

But special mention must be made of Charlie John F. Kennedy's Welsh Terrier.

At the height of the Cold War, during the Cuban Missile Crisis in 1962, the fate of the world hung in the balance. The U.S. and Russia were on the brink of nuclear Armageddon, and relations between the two countries had reached a dangerous stand-off over Russian nuclear missiles stationed in Cuba, within striking distance of the U.S.

Amid the chaos and the tension of the negotiations with Russian leader Nikita Khrushchev, Kennedy had Charlie brought to the situation room to sit in his lap while the course of action was decided.

It is said that Charlie had a calming effect on the president, who soon took steps to de-escalate the situation and not blow up the entire world.

THANK YOU, CHARLIE.

TILLMAN
skateboarding dog

Quickly put this book down, grab your nearest internet, and search for 'Tillman the skateboarding dog'.

Do this.

Okay, as you've now seen, Tillman was a phenomenal English bulldog from California who loved skateboarding more than anything else. Did you see him pick that board up in his teeth, flip it with his two front paws, and fly off down the pavement, propelling himself at incredible speed with those short, powerful legs?

In 2009, Tillman gained a place in Guinness World Records, setting the fastest time for a 100m skate by a dog at 19.678 seconds.

Tillman's record was beaten in 2013 — by a fraction of a second — by Jumpy the Dog, a Border-Collie-mix rescue dog.

Jumpy is also undoubtedly an amazing dog.

But does Jumpy surf? Tillman spent his summers catching waves in his home territory of Southern California and sometimes even down in Mexico.

Sadly, Tillman passed away in 2015, survived by his loving owner, Ron Davis.

Google 'Tillman surfing' now.

THE SHE-WOLF

The She-Wolf. One of the most underappreciated dogs of all time. She saved, nursed, and nurtured the twin babies Romulus and Remus, who grew up to found a little city called ROME.

The She-Wolf is one of the most significant figures in the foundational myth of Rome. Born to Rhea Silvia, daughter of the ancient king Numitor, and the god Mars, the twins were seen as a threat by King Amulius, who had usurped Numitor on his way to taking the throne. And so King Amulius ordered the boys to be killed at birth, and they were left abandoned by the banks of the river Tiber.

But they didn't die. Instead, they were saved by the She-Wolf and taken into her den, a cave which came to be known as the Lupercal, where she cared for the young infants as if they were her own cubs.

They were found in the cave by the shepherd Faustulus, who adopted them and raised them as shepherds, oblivious to their royal heritage. The boys grew into leaders of a rebellion against King Amulius, each of them commanding an army of supporters.

When Amulius was killed in the uprising and Numitor returned to the throne, Romulus and Remus set about founding their own city. They couldn't agree on which hill to found the city though, so Romulus straight-up killed Remus and built Rome on his chosen hill, because humans are the worst.

Nonetheless, Rome would grow to become the centre of a sprawling empire, the world's oldest metropolis, and to be regarded by some as the birthplace of Western civilisation.

The image of Romulus and Remus suckling from the She-Wolf is one of history's most enduring motifs, and has inspired countless artworks.

But she doesn't even get a name. Just the 'She-Wolf'. Outrageous. What an amazing dog. She deserves better.

BUDDY

Buddy the German Shepherd was a very important and influential dog. She was the first seeing-eye dog in the U.S. and a pioneer of the Seeing Eye movement around the world.

In 1927, Morris Frank, who had lost the use of both eyes, came across a newspaper article, read to him by his father, written by Dorothy Harrison Eustis, a dog trainer living in Switzerland.

Eustis described a successful guide-dog program in Germany that was provided to World War I veterans who'd lost their sight. Morris hated being dependent on other people and knew immediately that this was something he needed to try. He wrote to Eustis, saying, 'I want one of those dogs!'. Eustis invited Morris to come to her dog-training school, Fortunate Fields, and Morris flew as soon as he could to Switzerland to be paired with a dog.

It was there that he met Buddy and was trained to work

with her. In 1928, he returned with Buddy to America, thrilled with his newfound independence, and, in 1929, along with Eustis, he founded the first U.S. Seeing Eye guide-dog school. Buddy and Morris travelled across America, advocating the use of guide dogs to aid the vision impaired and campaigning 'to get Buddy accepted all over America with no more fuss than if she were a cane'.

Because of Buddy and Morris, guide dogs are now permitted to travel on all passenger airlines, and are accepted into restaurants, hotels, trains, and many other public spaces that had previously banned guide dogs.

Morris said, 'Buddy delivered to me the divine gift of freedom,' and together they helped change the lives of millions. What a team.

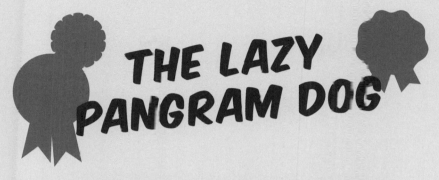

THE LAZY PANGRAM DOG

'The quick brown fox jumps over the lazy dog.'

Definitely the best pangram* of all time.

*A sentence that uses all 26 letters of the English language

SUSAN
the original corgi of Queen Elizabeth II

Pomp, ceremony, coronations, and corgis. The short, stocky, adorable herding dogs are as on-brand for the British monarch as Devonshire Tea and strange waving techniques.

Queen Elizabeth II's obsession with the Pembroke Welsh Corgi predates even her sixty-five year reign. Since 1933, corgis have been part of the British royal family; the first of them, Dookie, was owned by Elizabeth's parents, King George VI and Queen Elizabeth.

On her 18th birthday, her father gave Princess Elizabeth the two-month-old corgi, Susan.

Susan accompanied Elizabeth everywhere. The Queen even smuggled her along on her honeymoon with Prince Phillip in 1947. During her reign, The Queen has owned more than 30 corgis, most of them direct descendants of Susan, the original matriarch of the corgis of Windsor.

Susan ruled her domain with an iron paw, and was known for her propensity for snapping at the ankles of servants, on one occasion even biting a police officer.

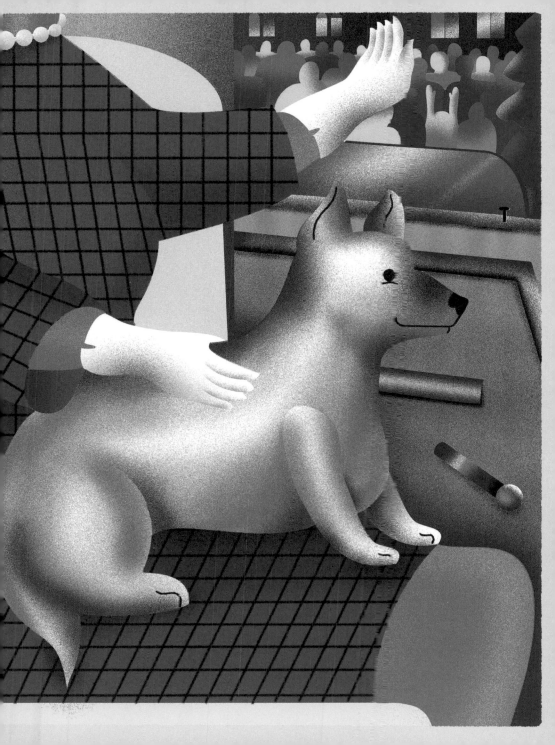

The royal corgis have for decades enjoyed the decadence and trappings of palace life, including a specially prepared chef-made menu.

Sadly, Willow, the final of the corgi line, died in 2018. The Queen had stopped breeding them so that they would not have to be rehomed when she herself is no longer around. Willow had appeared in a 2012 skit alongside The Queen and 007 actor Daniel Craig, which was filmed for the opening ceremony of the London Olympics.

The Queen still has two surviving Dorgis (Dachshund/ Pembroke Welsh Corgi crossbreeds), Vulcan (what a name), and Cider.

A distinguished era in British canine history has come to an end. Vale the long reign of the royal corgis.

Susan and Princess Elizabeth.

MARNIE
THE DOG

♡ Q

🔖

Marnie is an Instagram superstar with more than 2.1 million followers, and she is probably the best thing on the internet. Adopted from a rescue home at age 11, the 16-year-old Shih Tzu is instantly recognisable for her lopsided head and lolling tongue, which hangs preposterously and perpetually from one side of her mouth.

ARGOS

Argos was the faithful dog of Odysseus, the hero of Homer's *The Odyssey*.

In this epic poem, Odysseus returns home after 20 years of adventures — he was fighting the Trojan War for 10 years, and it took him another 10 years to get home, because traffic, gods, and monsters.

Odysseus returns to find his house in Ithaca taken over by suitors, vying for the hand of his wife, Penelope, and so he enters his old home disguised as a beggar.

Argos recognises his master, though. The old and faithful dog lies, ridden with fleas, on a pile of manure, his body wracked by time and neglect.

Odysseus had raised and trained Argos as a puppy, but had left for Troy before Argos was old enough to go hunting with him. As a young dog, Argos had been cared for by the men of Ithaca, and had gone with them on hunts for deer, wild boar, and hare. Argos had grown into a powerful hunter

with a keen nose, whose speed was unmatched.

But those days are long past. Now he lies forgotten and abandoned, left to wait patiently for his master.

He has waited two decades (an age in dog years) for Odysseus, and is so flooded with happiness and love and the emotion of it all that he manages to wag his tail excitedly and then promptly dies.

But that's not even the saddest part. It turns out that the faithful Argos had waited all of this time for a sadistic jerk. Once Odysseus defeats the suitors in a game of skill devised by Penelope, he sets about murdering them all before brutally torturing any of the house servants that he deems to have supported those suitors in his absence — remember, he'd been gone 20 years and they all thought he was dead.

And Odysseus and Penelope live happily ever after, basking in the warmth of their rekindled middle-aged romance and the glory of their slaughter.

Dogs are the real heroes.

LAIKA
the Soviet space dog

In 1957, *Sputnik II*, the second spacecraft to be sent into the Earth's orbit, was launched by the Soviet Union. The satellite was the first to carry a living animal, Laika, a stray dog plucked from the streets of Moscow for the mission.

The purpose was to measure the effects of spaceflight on living creatures and to figure out how humans might survive in space. There was no de-orbit plan though, so this was a death mission from the beginning.

Laika and Soviet spacecraft
Sputnik II pictured on a 1957
Mongolian postage stamp.

While the Soviets claimed that Laika survived for six days in orbit, until her oxygen ran out, the truth is that the poor thing died from overheating within hours of launch.

Monuments were erected to her, and her image adorned the faces of stamps, cigarettes, and other branded merchandise. She was held up as the embodiment of heroism and sacrifice for the advancement of humankind.

That's rubbish. Laika never asked to be sent to space to die a painful death.

She should, however, be remembered as one of the greatest dogs of all time, to serve as a reminder of man's cruel and ruthless ambition, and of the fact that shooting dogs into space is horrible.

Don't.

RIN TIN TIN

THIS DOG. This dog is incredible. Rin Tin Tin, the megastar German Shepherd of the silent film era, is perhaps the most famous dog of all time.

Orphaned in World War I and found in an abandoned German military kennel in France in 1918 by American GI Lee Duncan, Rin Tin Tin moved to the U.S. in 1919 as a war refugee.

Duncan formed a powerful bond with the athletic, talented, and genuinely expressive dog, whom he regarded as a good-luck charm and even considered invincible. Friends encouraged Duncan to enter Rin Tin Tin into dog shows, and in 1922, he wowed crowds at the Los Angeles Dog Show by making a winning leap of 11 feet 9 inches.

Rin Tin Tin was a very talented dog with excellent penmanship.

42

Duncan soon began pitching Rin Tin Tin as a film star to movie studios, and in 1922, he caught his first bit part in the *The Man from Hell's River*. Rin Tin Tin earned his first starring role the next year in *Where the North Begins*, and went on to star in 26 feature films for Warner Bros., mainly playing himself, as well as numerous radio specials. He was credited with single paw-edly keeping the film studio afloat for years, such was his box-office pull.

In August 1932, news of Rin Tin Tin's death was broadcast nationally — interrupting regular broadcasts — and made headlines around the world.

But his silver-screen lineage continues. Lee Duncan owned and trained four generations of German Shepherds named Rin Tin Tin, all direct descendants of the original. He never trademarked the name, and when he died in 1960, the tradition was passed on. There is a twelfth-generation descendant named Rin Tin Tin *still* starring in film and television today.

BOBBIE THE WONDER DOG

Look, with a name like Bobbie the Wonder Dog, this wonderful Scotch Collie from Silverton, Oregon, was probably always going to be a shoo-in for inclusion. But he really was an incredible dog.

In 1923, Bobbie was on a road trip in Indiana with his family — Frank and Elizabeth Brazier and their two daughters, Nova and Leona. At a rest stop, Bobbie was attacked by three dogs and chased off. The family looked everywhere for him to no avail, and eventually had to set off back home without him.

Six months later, a battered and exhausted Bobbie turned up on the doorstep of his family home. More than 2,500 miles away from where they had last seen him.

Bobbie had journeyed across the country, during winter no less, to find his way home, picking up the scent of his family at various places they'd stopped on their route.

The story made national news, and Bobbie shot to global fame. Reporters were able to piece together his travels by interviewing people who had seen him on his way home.

Bobbie had made friends right across the U.S., stopping in shantytowns and service stations, but always continuing on.

Bobbie was a superstar. He was everywhere. Bobbie the Wonder Dog.

Bobbie was given the key to the city of Portland, numerous medals, and a bejewelled collar. He was even given his own house (really).

When he died in 1927, Rin Tin Tin (another greatest dog) laid the wreath on Bobbie's grave, and the Mayor of Portland gave a eulogy at his funeral.

He was such a good boy.

RILEY
the birthday dog

There has never been a dog happier with himself and with his birthday cake than Riley.

When owner Maureen Ravelo posted this image of her Bichon Frise x Poodle posing in front of a cake on his birthday in 2010, the image quickly made it to Reddit and then went viral.

The meme has become shorthand for people too lazy to write a proper birthday message to their friends on social media, and also a representation of the very 'special' feeling one might feel after eating a really 'special' cake.

In a strange twist, the propaganda arm of the North Korean state media also picked up the image, spreading it as an example of American excess, claiming that while the poor of America starved, billionaire dogs were living (ahem) the life of Riley.

And while wealth disparity is a many-layered cake, Riley will remain refreshingly and perennially one-dimensional in his sleepy-eyed satisfaction.

Riley enjoying his birthday cake in 2010.

MOSCOW'S METRO DOGS

A train rattles to a halt at a train station. The automatic doors slide open. In steps a dog. She knows where she's going. She knows how to get there. She doesn't think she's people. She is dog. She's got trains to catch.

There are about 35,000 stray dogs on the streets of Moscow, and around 500 are estimated to be living in the city's train stations. However, a group of around 20 of them have learned to successfully navigate the Moscow Metro system.

Statue of Malchik, one of Moscow's most beloved train-riding dogs.

They have memorised timetables and recognise stations by scent, by the place names announced over loudspeakers, and even by the individual voices of station announcers.

The canny canines have co-evolved with humans, learning their signals, recognising who will most likely give them a treat, and ascertaining the best carriages to have a nap in and stay warm and safe.

They've become a much-loved part of the city to Moscow's residents. When one of the dogs, Malchik, was stabbed to death in 2001, shocked residents raised funds to erect a statue in his memory, which now sits at the entrance to Mendeleyevskaya train station.

SOPHIE TUCKER

In 2009, Jan Griffith was out sailing with her family and their Cattle Dog, Sophie Tucker, off the coast of Queensland, Australia, when their boat hit rough waters.

Sophie was thrown overboard, and in the chaos the Griffith family was unable to save her. They returned home mourning the loss of their beloved pup ... until four months later, when Sophie made her miraculous and triumphant return home.

Sophie had survived, doggy-paddling five nautical miles through shark-infested waters to nearby St Bees Island. To stave off starvation, Sophie hunted wild goats on the island and presumably had heaps of adventures. Rangers spotted her on the island and managed to capture her before bringing her back home to her family, where she bowled them over with joy upon arrival.

BARRY
the Saint Bernard Rescue Dog

On the Italian–Swiss border, between Mont Blanc and Monte Rosa, is the Great St Bernard Pass, one of the oldest passes through the Western Alps. And at the highest point of the pass sits the Great St Bernard Hospice, a hostel and monastery, which has for almost 1,000 years provided safe haven to road-weary travellers, shelter from the elements, and protection from roving bandits.

At some point between 1660 and 1670, the monastery began breeding dogs, first as guard dogs and later to accompany trekkers through the treacherous snowy peaks. A mixture of Mastiff, French Bulldog, Asiatic hound, and local farm dog, the broad-shouldered breed made the perfect trailblazer, ploughing through thick snowdrifts. Their phenomenal noses and strength also made them perfect rescue dogs.

The most famous of them is Barry.

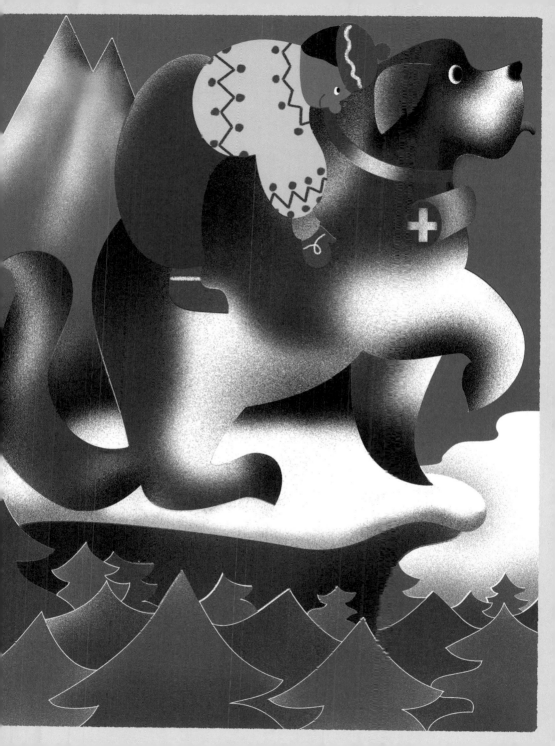

Born in 1800, over his lifetime at the Hospice, Barry was said to have rescued at least 40 lost wanderers, tracking them through blizzards, venturing into deep crevasses, using his own body heat to warm them up until help arrived. Barry was even said to have dragged a small lost child down a mountain and back to the Hospice, licking his face to keep him warm along the way.

Such was Barry's fame that the dogs of the Hospice were simply known as 'Barry dogs'. This may also be because Barry is such a fantastic name for a dog.

In 1880, the breed would officially become known as the Saint Bernard, but the original rescue dogs of the Hospice were slightly smaller and shorter-haired than the hulking, slobbering, modern beauties of the *Beethoven* films.

And while the image of the Saint Bernard rescue dogs carrying small barrels of brandy or wine from their collars is one that has endured throughout history, this almost certainly never happened. Mixing alcohol and hypothermia is, frankly, a terrible idea. But the dream of a great jowly dog who will not only save your life but also deliver booze in the process is a dream that is simply too good to snuff out. So carry on with that, everyone.

Jan van Eyck's
THE ARNOLFINI PORTRAIT DOG

Jan van Eyck's 1434 oil painting, *The Arnolfini Portrait*, of Giovanni Arnolfini and his wife, who was possibly named Costanza, is widely regarded as one of the most influential and original paintings of its era.

Many will point to the painting's near-perfect orthogonal perspective, its intricate and rich detail, and its complex iconography.

Jan van Eyck's *The Arnolfini Portrait*, 1434.

Or to the use of the convex mirror in the background, said to signify the all-seeing eye of God, but which also expands the space to the viewer, taking them behind the painting, breaking the fourth wall and revealing — in a radical gesture of self-reflexivity — the artist himself.

But look towards the bottom of the frame. Regard the newlywed couple's small yet breathtaking dog — a symbol at the time of wealth and status, and of endless love devotion, and fidelity. Look at its exquisitely detailed coat, its eyes deep, shimmery pools that seem to gaze back into your very soul and say: 'I see you. I love you. Everything is going to be fine.'

Truly majestic.

CYLART
greyhound of
Llywelyn the Great

Please brace yourself for a tragedy of epic proportions.

Rising to power in 1200 AD as ruler of the Welsh kingdom of Gwynned, Prince Llywelyn the Great was one of Wales's longest-reigning and most successful leaders. Llywelyn was given a young greyhound named Cylart by King John of England as thanks for his help in a military campaign against Scotland. As the Prince of Wales's power grew, however, the relationship with England soured, and soon the two kingdoms were at war.

Cylart was a perceptive companion, picking up on the prince's mood and growling at adversaries when discussions became heated. The greyhound was also deeply protective of the prince's infant son, Dafydd.

In 1210 AD, while the prince was travelling with his young son and a group of soldiers, they came across signs that there were English raiders nearby and went to investigate. As it was not safe to bring Dafydd with them, the baby was left in a secluded tent, with trusty Cylart standing guard.

After a bloody skirmish in which they saw off the English raiders, Llywelyn and his men returned to camp, with the prince, brooding from the battle, heading immediately to his tent to check on baby Dafydd. As he entered the tent he saw Cylart sitting by Daffyd's crib. But instead of running as usual to greet his master, Cylart remained panting beside the baby's crib. Blood dripped from Cylart's jaws and gore stained his matted fur. In an instant, Llywelyn assessed the terrible scene before him, bellowing 'Cylart! You have killed my son!' and hurling his spear at the greyhound, who made no effort to leap out of the way. As Cylart lay dying on the tent floor, the prince ran to Dafydd's crib, pulling off the blanket. But the baby lay unharmed.

It was then that Llywelyn noticed it — the hulking body of a dead wolf. The great beast lay mauled at the other side of the tent. The blood on Cylart's jaws was that of the wolf. His fur was matted from injuries sustained protecting baby Daffyd. Realisation and remorse flooded through the prince as he raced back to the mortally wounded Cylart. Even as the life drained out of him, the greyhound managed to lick his master's face and hands in one final act of unconditional love.

You were warned.

As with all legends, there is debate surrounding the story of Cylart's origin and even his name. He's often referred to

When St Roch (left), the patron saint of dogs and dog lovers, contracted the plague, St Guinefort (right) is said to have nursed him back to health by delivering bread and licking the wounds on his plague-infested leg. Next-level devotion.

as Gelert, Gellert, or Killhart. An enterprising tavern owner in Wales claimed that the grave of Gelert was inside his pub, which became an instant tourist hot spot, and helped popularise the name Gelert.

And there are striking similarities between the story of Cylart and St Guinefort, an actual dog SAINT of early Catholicism who was said to have saved the child of a knight of Lyon, France, from the jaws of a snake, only to be killed by the knight.

But whoever he was, he was definitely a great dog.

Further reading on Cylart: *The Pawprints of History: Dogs and the Course of Human Events* (2002) by Stanley Coren.

Chilean reforestation Border Collies
DAS, OLIVIA, AND SUMMER

There are videos of them on Facebook and Instagram. Three Border Collies, bounding joyfully across charred earth and between blackened pine trunks, each strapped with custom-made backpacks, clouds of seed trailing behind them. Their happiness is pure and palpable.

In 2017, Chile suffered its worst fire season on record, with forest fires ripping across 1.4 million acres, much of it native forest, and destroying more than 1,500 homes.

Several months later, Border Collies Das and her daughters Olivia and Summer began aiding the reforestation effort in a unique and ingenious way.

The three dogs are trained to race through the burnt-out forestland, spreading native seeds as they go. Their owners, sisters Francisca and Constanza Torres, reward them with treats for each full backpack scattered through the forest. On a good day, the collies can cover 30 kilometres of ground, spreading 10 kilograms of seeds. And while the dogs are in it for the thrill of the race and the treats, they also absolutely love their very important job.

Kate Bush

The Hounds of Love

Relaxation tip:

Close your eyes, take deep breaths, and imagine yourself in the forest. Das and Olivia and Summer are there, too. That song by Kate Bush is playing. But don't run away from these hounds of love, run with them. Run through the trees. Imagine the forest growing around you. You are a dog now. Feels good, no?

NICK CARTER
dog detective

Nick Carter is an American musician and actor best known as one of the founding members of the multi-platinum-record-selling boy-band Backstreet Boys. He is also not a dog. This is also not that Nick Carter.

In the early 1900s, the most famous Nick Carter in America was a keen-nosed, droopy-eyed bloodhound, named after a popular dime-novel detective.

Born in late 1899, he was a legendary police tracker dog, who, with handler Captain G.V. Mullikin, is credited with tracking down more than 650 missing persons and criminals.

Such was Nick's fame that huge crowds would turn out just to see him work when he was on the job

Nick was particularly good at picking up cold scents, and in one case managed to pick up a trail more than 12 days old. He once tracked a suspect more than 55 miles. That's a really long way. He just loved finding people and solving crimes so much.

Neighbours. The iconic Australian soapie, which follows the highs and lows in the lives of a group of families and residents of the fictitious Ramsay Street, is the longest-running Australian drama series. It helped launch the careers of Kylie Minogue, Guy Pearce, Russell Crowe, Margot Robbie, and Natalie Imbruglia.

It's one of Australia's most successful and enduring cultural exports, much to the bewilderment of some, who are astounded that the grinding monotony of middle-class Australian suburbia, with some flourishes of high drama (seemingly every long-running character has suffered total, immediate amnesia and/or returned from the dead at some point), could strike such a chord internationally. But the show's beauty lies in its banal familiarity — the type of show that you could literally watch after 25 years and still have an idea of what's going on.

In 1987, a gorgeous Labrador named Bouncer joined the cast and bounded onto the television screens and into the hearts of millions of viewers around the world.

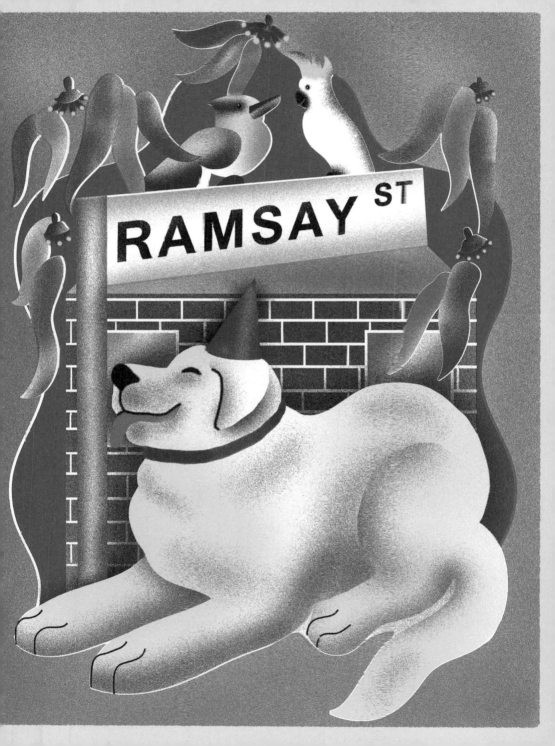

Bouncer quickly became one of the most loved dogs in soapie history and was reportedly paid more than any of the human cast members, pulling in between $100,000 and $200,000 per season.

Bouncer was a paragon of joyful heroism. He answered the phone. He saved Madge Bishop from a kitchen fire (by calling emergency services). He befriended Mrs Mangel, Ramsay Street's resident super-villain, seeing past her frosty exterior and into the heart of a lonely old woman who just wanted to be loved. Then he knocked her off a ladder, giving her total and immediate amnesia.

But the scene that Bouncer will forever be remembered for is one of the strangest in the series' history. While watching the wedding video of Joe Mangel and Kerry Bishop, Bouncer drifts off to sleep. The scene shifts to INSIDE his dream. He's wearing a tie. He's getting married to Rosie, the Border Collie from next door. Distorted wedding bells ring, panpipes play, the focus is soft, and the scene awash with fake flowers, rainbows, and streamers. The two dogs prance and play together. The camera pans across fake rolling hills and back to the newlyweds, now with a litter of newborn puppies, settling into a kennel with the words HOME SWEET HOME stuck above the door.

The immediate question that springs to mind upon viewing is 'how did this ever happen?'. Well, a screenwriter who worked on *Neighbours* through the 1990s and into the 2000s, and who had just joined the writing team in 1990, answered that question.

'I'm pretty sure that came to me on an LSD trip. And I pitched it at work and it got accepted. Go figure. The dumb, fun, stupid shit you do when you're young and you've just casually been chatting to God.'

Which makes perfect sense. It's off the wall. It's totally cooked. And its a high-water mark in Australian television history. It's the moment the writers threw realism to the dogs. Anything could happen from then on. Cue car-wrecks, plane crashes, bombings, disappearances, reappearances, and many, many more cases of complete and immediate amnesia.

Bouncer left *Neighbours* in 1993 and died of cancer 13 weeks later. He received more tributes from fans than any other cast member in the show's history.

ASHLEY WHIPPET

the first disc dog

Ashley Whippet (real name, real Whippet) was the soaring, leaping, acrobatic genius of a dog that, with his best friend, Alex, founded an entire sport and captured the heart of a nation.

On 5 August 1974, Alex Stein, a 19-year-old college student from Ohio State University, took his beloved Ashley Whippet and a Frisbee into Dodger Stadium during a televised baseball game between the Los Angeles Dodgers and Cincinnati Reds. Just as players had finished warming up, and moments before the game was to commence, Alex lofted the Frisbee onto the pitch. Instantly, Ashley raced down the stand and leapt over the fence and onto the field, catching the disc in his jaws before it hit the ground. Alex was next to jump the fence, joining Ashley on the pitch and throwing the Frisbee again as the Whippet chased the disc at 35 miles per hour, leaping nine feet high and cutting spectacular, graceful shapes as he snatched it from the air in front of the packed and confused stadium.

The crowd and players were so awed by Ashley's disc skills that play halted entirely, while announcer Joe Garagiola continued to commentate as the duo performed. A full eight minutes went by before security finally ushered Alex and Ashley off the field, and Alex was arrested (later released after paying a small fine). And thus the world's first disc-dog launched himself into the national consciousness.

Ashley and Alex would go on to perform on *The Tonight Show*; *Sports Illustrated* would label Ashley 'the surest jaws on all fours' and the pair performed on the White House lawn for the Carter administration. In 1975, due to the sudden media attention, the World Frisbee Championships launched a canine division, which Ashley won three years in a row. The competition would later become known as the Ashley Whippet Invitational, now a global series with divisions across Europe, Japan, and China. There's even an Ashley Whippet Museum in Naperville, Illinois. In 1999, *USA Today* recognised Ashley as one of the Great Athletic Animals of the twentieth century.

Ashley died of cancer in Alex's arms at the age of 13. But what a story. And what a legacy.

Ashley Whippet soaring.

ANUBIS

In Egyptian mythology, Anubis, son of the Sun God Ra, was the dog- or jackal-headed Lord of the Dead and the god of embalming and mummification, sometimes represented only as a sleek black dog. He was worshipped as a guide for the dead, protecting them on their journey to the Underworld. Anubis was also believed to the Guardian of the Scales, who would weigh the hearts of souls seeking entrance into the Underworld against Ma'at, the goddess and personification of truth and justice, who was represented on the scales as an ostrich feather. Those with hearts lighter than the feather would gain entrance to the Underworld, and those with heavy hearts would be devoured by the demoness Ammit.

So he was a fairly impressive dog in the scheme of it all. Transcendent, even.

ABUWTIYUW

Abuwtiyuw is the earliest-known named domesticated pet, and he lived during the Sixth Dynasty of Ancient Egypt, sometime between 2135 and 2181 BC. He was also a dog.

In 1935, Egyptologist George A. Reisner and his expedition photographer, Mohammedani Ibrahim, uncovered a white limestone tablet that had been built into the structure of an ancient Pharaonic-era tomb in the Giza Necropolis.

The tablet describes Abuwtiyuw. The royal guard dog of an unknown pharaoh. A noble hound with pointed ears and curly tail, similar in appearance to a greyhound.

Burials for dogs in Ancient Egypt were not uncommon. Dogs were often buried with their master. Abuwtiyuw died before his master, though, and was given the equivalent of a state funeral. While his tomb has not been found (the tablet was used in a separate tomb at a later date), his burial appears to have been particularly elaborate, replete with an ornate coffin from the royal treasury, funerary gifts, and a tomb built by gangs of masons.

'His Majesty did this for him in order that he (the dog) might be Honoured (before the great god, Anubis),' the inscription reads.

What amazing feats did he perform? What heroic deeds? We don't know. But all signs point to the fact that Abuwtiyuw was a truly exceptional dog.

CHAMPION TICKLE EM JOCK

Champion Tickle Em Jock was a stunning Scottish Terrier, owned by Andrew Albright Jr., and the winner of the 'Best in Show' award at the 1911 Westminster Kennel Club Dog Show. No mean feat, given that the breed was viewed by dog-show types at the time as being inferior, and other dog owners at the event had even complained about his inclusion, accusing him of 'lacking the qualities of a typical Scottish Terrier'. He was the first of his breed to win the title.

He was an outsider. It was an upset. An outrage.

Imagine, if you will, the reactions of the audience members of the 1911 Westminster Kennel Club Dog Show. Of the competing dog owners. Cast your mind's eye across the crowd as his win is announced and see the spectacles falling from stunned, widened eyes. The pipes tumbling from slack jaws, agape in horror.

Hear the shocked gasps. The rippling murmurs.

Now imagine, later that same year, Jock biting the hand of a judge at the Monmouth County Kennel Club Dog Show, immediately after winning the best-in-breed award.

Because that's exactly what he did. He was a champion who played by his own rules. He stuck it to high society. And it was delicious.

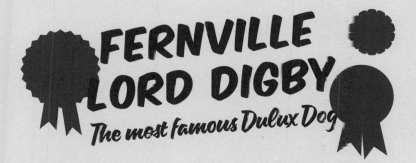

FERNVILLE LORD DIGBY
The most famous Dulux Dog

In 1961, the household paint brand Dulux launched an advertising icon. The 'Dulux Dog' was an Old English Sheepdog named Dash, and the idea was that by placing a tin of paint next to a magnificent dog, people would be compelled to buy that paint. And it worked.

The advertising campaign was so successful that the term Dulux Dog would become synonymous with the breed. The most famous of the Dulux Dogs was Fernville Lord Digby, which is possibly the most excellent name for a dog ever. In the more than fifty years since the campaign launched, many Old English Sheepdogs have starred in Dulux's commercials, but none with as much grace or class as Fernville Lord Digby. The great grey-and-white shaggy-haired wonder — who was trained by celebrity dog handlers Cynthia and Norman Harrison — was so good at encouraging people to decorate their homes that he had his own private chauffeur to take him to and from the studio, had three body doubles, and even went on to star in his own 1973 film, *Digby, The Biggest Dog in the World*, co-starring Jim Dale and Spike Milligan.

BALTO

Balto. Glorious Balto. The brave Siberian Husky is the only dog to have a statue commemorating him in New York City. The inscription below the bronze in Central Park reads:

> **'Dedicated to the indomitable spirit of the sled dogs that relayed antitoxin 600 miles over rough ice, across treacherous waters, through arctic blizzards, from Nenana to the relief of stricken Nome in the winter of 1925.'**

The story of Balto and the Great Race for Mercy is so extraordinary, you wouldn't read about it. But go on, read about it.

In the deep dark of winter in the small town of Nome, Alaska, an outbreak of diphtheria was detected, spreading through the town's children. In 1925, diphtheria was a serious threat, often fatal in children, and the only hope of holding off a major and very deadly epidemic was a serum stored in Anchorage, more than 800 miles south.

Pack ice prohibited delivery by ship, and the only aeroplane capable of making the journey was immobilised

by the winter freeze. A train could deliver a cargo of antitoxin part of the way to the town of Nenana, but this still left 674 miles of rugged and icy wilderness to Nome. Such a trip would usually take 30 days, but because of the terrible conditions, it was estimated that the serum would only last six.

A hasty decision was made. A sled-dog relay of 20 mushers (sled-dog drivers) and 150 dogs would relay the serum from Nenana to Nome, up the Iditarod Trail, changing at a series of checkpoints along the way.

Balto led the final team of dogs through temperatures that plummeted below -50 degrees Fahrenheit. The trail was treacherous and visibility was abysmal. Driven by Gunnar Kaasen, the team made its way to the checkpoint ahead of schedule but found the awaiting team still sleeping, and so pressed on. Through a raging blizzard and pitch-darkness, Balto was somehow able to stick to the trail and lead the team into Nome. The town was saved.

The teams had made the journey in a little over five days. None of the vials of serum had broken along the way.

If this all sounds to you like the plot to a nail-biting action film, you are correct. Many movies have been made about the race, including the Disney animation *Balto*, loosely based on the mission, in which Balto was voiced by Kevin Bacon. Meaning that not only is Balto one of the most heroic, loyal, and determined dogs of all time, but he is also only one degree of separation from Kevin Bacon.

SINBAD

Sinbad the sailing dog spent 11 years aboard USCGC *Campbell* from 1937–1948. In his time on the ship, he attained the rank of Chief Dog — an actual rank — which was equivalent to Chief Petty Officer.

He was originally purchased by the ship's Chief Boatswain's Mate, as a gift for his girlfriend; however, her apartment building's ban on dogs meant that Sinbad was unable to stay with her. The crew had become attached to Sinbad, though, and in a creative effort to keep him on the ship, they enlisted the dog, making him a verified member of the U.S. Coast Guard, and justified his enlistment by saying that he displayed the characteristics of a regular sailor: drinking coffee and whiskey.

Sinbad (above) and aboard USCGC *Campbell* with crew (opposite).

Sinbad was assigned his own bunk and kept a watch shift. He also saw action during World War II, when the *Campbell* came under attack by enemy aircraft, and he was aboard when the ship rammed and sank a German U-Boat.

Sinbad would become a regular presence in local bars when the *Campbell* stopped in port, and he soon became a media sensation, with photographs and features in newspapers around the U.S. and worldwide.

While generally he was a great sailor and beloved crew member, Sinbad also played by his own rules and was demoted several times for misbehaviour. He caused a 'diplomatic situation' and was banned from the island nation of Greenland for getting up the noses of local sheep farmers by frightening their stock while on port leave.

DOG OF OSU
a loyal dog of Korean folklore

The legendary loyalty of dogs is a frequent thread through Korean literature and mythology, with monuments to the most virtuous hounds not uncommon.

In fact, in Osu-myun, in the south-west of South Korea, there's an entire park dedicated to them, with statues of Balto, Hachikō, and Barry the Saint Bernard. A wondrous place. A place not unlike this book, but in park form.

The town is also the home of the Monument for the Loyal Dog, honouring one of the most famous dogs of Korean folklore.

In the folk tale of 'The Righteous Dog from Osu', written in 1230 AD, Kim Kae In was returning from a party with his dog, a burly but gentle Tibetan Mastiff, whose name time has forgotten. Kim was quite drunk, and lay down on the grass and fell into a deep sleep. While he was sleeping, a forest fire started in the woods nearby, which was soon raging towards the slumbering Kim. Kim's dog tried desperately to rouse him, barking and biting at his clothing. The flames were soon lapping right up beside them.

The dog dashed to a nearby stream to soak his long shaggy coat in its waters and raced back to Kim, wetting the grass around him and protecting him from the flames. Again and again the dog did this, until the fire had passed. Kim awoke soon after to find the dog beside him, dead from heat and exhaustion. Filled with grief and sorrow, Kim buried the dog nearby, placing his stave at the grave's head. From the stave a large tree grew, which still stands today. The region came to be known as Osu, meaning 'the tree of a dog', and the dog is remembered simply as the Dog of Osu.

LOLABELLE

Heart of a Dog is a lucid dream of a film made by avant-garde musician, composer, writer, and director Laurie Anderson in 2015.

At its centre is the story of Lolabelle, a Rat Terrier adopted by Anderson and her late husband, Lou Reed.

It shouldn't be surprising that a dog who belonged to two of a generation's most celebrated, boundary-bending artists was encouraged to explore her creative side, but Lolabelle's artistic output was phenomenal.

Lolabelle accompanied Anderson into the recording studio where she would stay for hours, endlessly entertained by the recording process. Anderson taught Lolabelle to paint with her claws by scratching shapes onto plastic sheets, using static electricity, and to make sculptures from her moulded paw prints. When Lolabelle went blind, her trainer, Elisabeth Weiss, taught her to play the piano. She played at charity shows. Released a Christmas album.

'We learned to love Lola as she learned to love us; with a tenderness we didn't know we had.'

While it touches the edges of absurdity in a wonderful way, the film is also a meditation on life, death, love, grief, and the afterlife. All inspired by a dog.

ELWOOD

There's a story that the original definition of the word 'cute' was 'ugly but interesting', and that its use to mean 'attractive' or 'adorable' is relatively modern. That's not actually true. The word cute originates from 'acute', meaning intense, keen, or clever.

By any definition, Elwood was one of the 'cutest' dogs of all time. The winner of the 2007 World's Ugliest Dog Contest, Elwood was mostly hairless, save for an electric streak of white hair across his head. His enormous tongue too big to fit in his mouth, lolled out of it, and he made strange sounds when he breathed.

The Chihuahua–Chinese-crested cross was adopted by his owner, Karen Quigley, from a rescue home in New Jersey, after he'd escaped being put down by a breeder who felt that he was too ugly to sell.

After winning the title, Elwood appeared in newspapers, on TV, and in magazines around the world. Karen used Elwood's newfound fame to advocate for adopting dogs from rescue homes: to her, the contest was not mean-spirited but instead proved that even the most different-looking animals can find loving, nurturing homes.

Karen even wrote a children's book about Elwood called *Everyone Loves Elwood*. And they did.

BUD NELSON

In 1903, while being rich and bored at a gentlemen's club in San Francisco, Dr Horatio Nelson Jackson, a physician from Burlington, Vermont, accepted a wager to prove that a four-wheeled automobile could be driven across the U.S. At the time, cars were rickety playthings for the super-wealthy, but Horatio accepted despite having no real driving experience, or even owning a car, because gentlemen's clubs are places for rich, bored men to go and accept ridiculous bets. If this all sounds annoying, read on — a dog is coming!

Horatio immediately bought a Winton two-cylinder, 20hp automobile, which he named *Vermont* after his hometown, and, with no mechanical experience, he hired a young mechanic named Sewell K. Crocker to accompany him.

The pair were beset by mechanical woes from the get-go. A tyre burst on the first day; the driving lanterns needed replacing on the second night.

Outside of Idaho, Horatio bought a bulldog named Bud, who would travel with them for the rest of the journey. It was at this point that the media became interested and the trio shot to fame, because their story now had a dog in it.

Journalists and fans would come out to see Bud at every stop along the way.

Bud loved riding up in the front of the car, and immediately took to life on the road; however, as he was allergic to the dust of the alkali flats, Horatio bought him a pair of driving goggles to protect his sensitive eyes. Their fame skyrocketed, because now the story had a dog wearing driving goggles in it. Bud appeared on the covers of magazines and newspapers all over the country.

After 63 days on the road, Bud, Horatio, and Sewell pulled into New York, completing the first journey across North America by car. Horatio won the $50 bet. He had spent more than $8,000 by the journey's end. Bud's goggles are now displayed in the Smithsonian Museum.

If you want to make a story interesting, put a dog in it. If you want to make it incredible, put goggles on the dog.

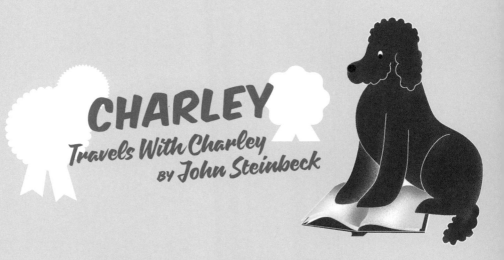

CHARLEY

Travels With Charley
BY John Steinbeck

Bud and Horatio did it first in 1903, and before long, the idea of jumping in a car with a dog and heading out across the country on a journey of discovery and rediscovery would become a well-worn cliché. But if you're going to do it, do it right.

John Steinbeck, the Nobel Prize-winning author of *The Grapes of Wrath*, *East of Eden*, and *Of Mice and Men*, realised at the age of 58, with his health faltering from heavy drinking and hard living, that while he'd spent a life writing about America, he'd never seen much of it.

So he packed a pick-up truck, which he'd converted into a caravan, and took off on a 10,000-mile journey through 37 U.S. states and Canada. With him he took Charley, his calm and gentle Standard Poodle, who would be his only companion on the trip.

Steinbeck observed that, in 1960, America was a nation driven by fear. It was the height of the Cold War, and the election campaign between John F. Kennedy and Richard Nixon was in full swing; the nation was divided.

With no one else on the road to talk to, Steinbeck talked to Charley, discussing trivial matters but also engaging in deep conversations about the racial prejudice and discrimination he witnessed in the deep South, his excitement at the progress being made in other regions of the country, and the tension between progress and nostalgia. And Charley listened, a silent psychologist in the passenger seat.

This striking, good-natured poodle, a rare breed in many states at the time, was also the perfect ambassador. Through Charley, Steinbeck met a host of strangers on the road from all walks of life, discussing with them their views on the country and the world.

The result of the trip, *Travels with Charley*, was published in 1962. It became an instant bestseller, celebrated as a classic of travel writing and memoir, and as a deeply insightful portrait of a country both on the brink of great social change and afraid of its future. A few months after its publication, Steinbeck was awarded the Nobel Prize for Literature.

That's not to say that Charley had anything to do with Steinbeck picking up the most coveted award in the literary world, but … actually, screw it. Charley was solely responsible for this.

Acknowledgements

Molly Dyson is one of my favourite artists and an all-round legend, so it is such a privilege to be sharing a title page with her. On the tightest of deadlines, Molly filled this book with the most beautiful, strange, and stunning dogs I have seen. Thank you, Molly! My employer and publisher, Scribe Publications, took a staff-meeting joke and follow-up proposal and ran with it. Ran with it so, so far. Now it's an actual book. Thanks to Marika Webb-Pullman (my wonderful editor) and Miriam Rosenbloom, who said yes to this; Laura Thomas, for her incredible design work; Allison Colpoys, for her art direction; Mick Pilkington, for production management; and all at Scribe and Scribe UK, for their amazing trust and enthusiasm for this gag. My friends Evan, Perrin, Isabel, Iolanthe, and Esther sent me heaps of messages about dogs. So did my dad, Andrew. Malisha Rama read heaps of my text messages about dogs and laughed at most of them. My grandmother Dr Jan Penney sent me a whole spreadsheet of them and gave the most excellent research advice. My housemates Bron, Mim, and Emily put up with my interesting mood arrangements around deadline time. My late (always) mum, Adani would have found it all really funny. Thanks to all the dogs that I have ever met and those that I haven't as well. You're all bloody great.

Scribe Publications
18–20 Edward St, Brunswick, Victoria 3056, Australia
2 John St, Clerkenwell, London, WC1N 2ES, United Kingdom
3754 Pleasant Ave, Suite 100, Minneapolis, Minnesota 55409 USA

Published by Scribe 2018

Photos: **page 2** Hercules sculpture photo by Cromagnon/Shutterstock.com; **page 7** Greyfriars Bobby sculpture photo by alice-photo/Shutterstock.com; **page 14** Hachiko one year anniversary from 'Showa Day by Day' volume 4, Kodansha Co., 1989.; **page 19** Mayor Brynneth Pawltro from facebook.com/brynneth.pawltro; **page 20** Mayor Max from mayormax.com; **page 34** 'Princess Elizabeth with her dog Sue' by Lisa Sheridan/Stringer, from the Hulton Royals Collection/Getty Images; **page 39** Mongolian stamp Michael Seleznev/Alamy Stock Photo; **page 42** Rin Tin Tin promotional photo by Chappel Bros. Inc, Rockford, IL.; **page 47** 'Riley the birthday dog' by Maureen Ravelo; **page 48** Malchik sculpture photo by TAR-TASS News Agency/Alamy Stock Photo; **pages 56-57** Jan van Eyck, Portrait of Giovanni(?) Arnolfini and his Wife © The National Gallery, London; **page 61** Saint Roch sculpture courtesy The Cloisters Collection, 1925; **page 64** Chilean Reforestation dog by AFP Contributor/Getty Images; **pages 70-73** photos courtesy the Ashley Whippet Museum; **pages 86-87** Sinbad publicity photos from Wikipedia/US Coast Guard.

Every effort has been made to trace copyright holders and to obtain their permission for the use of copyright material. The publisher apologises for any errors or omissions in the above list and would be grateful if notified of any corrections that should be incorporated in future reprints or editions of this book.

The moral rights of the author and illustrator have been asserted.

Printed and bound in China by 1010 Printing Co Ltd

Scribe Publications is committed to the sustainable use of natural resources and the use of paper products made responsibly from those resources.

9781925713510 (Australian edition)
9781911617648 (UK edition)
9781947534575 (US edition)

CiP records for this title are available from the National Library of Australia and the British Library.

scribepublications.com.au
scribepublications.co.uk
scribepublications.com